ABE LINCOLN
GOES TO WASHINGTON

— 1837-1865 —

Written and illustrated by Cheryl Harness

**NATIONAL
GEOGRAPHIC
SOCIETY**

Washington, D.C.

To Laura

I wish to acknowledge the assistance of Michael R. Maione,
Historian, Ford's Theatre National Historic Site,
Edwin Bearss, Chief Historian Emeritus, National Park Service,
Carl Mehler, National Geographic Society Map Editor
for the Book Division, Joseph F. Ochlak, Map Researcher,
the support of my editor Barbara Lalicki, and the inspiration
found in the lives of Abe and Mary and in the book
by Jack Finney, *Time and Again.*

I think: If I stare hard enough at these black-and-white pictures of a long-ago President, can I get those gloomy eyes to crinkle into a smile? Hear his voice? What did that wide mouth look like when he laughed? How did the living, colorful Lincoln really look, walking down a dusty road?

What was on your mind, Abe, when your picture was taken? When you left the photographer's studio, put your tall hat on your head, what did the street full of horses and buggies, and folks thinking about the Civil War or what's-for-dinner *look* like—*sound* like—*smell* like?

Books are a time machine. Pictures are the key, imagination's the fuel, and I set off to find Mr. Lincoln and his times back upstream in the vanished past.

On an April evening in 1837, a tall, lanky fellow swung down from his mud-spattered horse. He'd come 18 miles along the Sangamon River from the village of New Salem to the town of Springfield, Illinois.

The young man was a representative in the State Legislature where he had worked to make Springfield the new state capital. He was a new lawyer, too, and he had the papers to prove it—tucked in his tall stovepipe hat. All of his books and clothes were stuffed in his saddlebags.

When he had carried them up the narrow, wooden stairs to a room over the general store, 28-year-old Abraham Lincoln was settled in his new hometown, there to seek his fortune.

When folks got in legal trouble with land or money, murder or romance, they might come to the law office Abe shared with his partner, John T. Stuart. Abe practiced politics, too, and folks came to hear his speeches. His was a fast-growing county that needed good roads and canals, Abe argued, and strong laws. There was a "spirit of violence" in the land where a man like Elijah Lovejoy of Alton, Illinois, could be killed and get his printing press thrown in the Mississippi River just because he had Yankee anti-slavery opinions.

"Depend on it," Abe said, if people can do such things and get away with it, "this government cannot last."

Writing, talking politics, and visiting folks as he traveled between county courthouses, young Abe Lincoln was making a name for himself.

One December night in 1839, Abe slicked down his hair, shined his shoes, and went to a ball.

There he was introduced to Miss Mary Todd from Lexington.

Abe felt miserably shy and gangly as he bowed to the pretty Kentucky lady. She smiled gaily as she fluttered her fan and asked, "Do you dance, Mr. Lincoln?"

As they whirled about the polished floor, Mary talked with Abe about books and politics. They soon forgot about his clumsy feet.

And so they began courting. They argued and broke up, made up, broke up, and were finally married on November 4, 1842.

Abe had these words engraved on Mary's ring: "Love is eternal."

The Lincoln house was enlarged to two stories in 1856.

By 1844, Abe and Mary were able to buy a house. It sat at the corner of 8th and Jackson Streets. Lawyer Lincoln was getting to be known as a man whose ambitions and ideas were extending beyond Illinois. In 1846, he was elected to the United States House of Representatives.

The Lincolns left their quiet corner in Springfield. They took their children, four-year-old Robert and baby Edward, on trains, steamboats, and carriages to Washington, D.C.

After only one term, Abe and his family came back home to Illinois. He felt like a failure in politics. He and his political party, the Whigs, hadn't agreed with President Polk's popular Mexican War that had won western land, such as California, for the United States.

Abe took up lawyering again.

In 1850, the Lincolns' younger son, Edward, died, and a new baby was born. Abe and Mary named him William. In 1853, their last child was born. Abe called baby Thomas, "Tad."

Abe liked to take his two little boys with him to his law office. Tad and Willie made paper hats, spilled the ink bottles, and stuck pencils in the spittoons. The neighbors smiled out the windows to see long-legged Abe walking home with a bratty boy under each arm.

In Abe Lincoln's America, there was a monster. It was known as "the slavery question." In the South it was legal to buy and sell black people as slaves. Would slavery be allowed in the new states and territories in the West? That's where thousands of folks were going, shoving the Indians out of the way to get open land and California gold. More and more Northerners were saying, "No!" They didn't want slavery to spread. Some wanted slavery to end.

The slavery question was about the rights of black human beings. Were they entitled to the rights and protections in the Declaration of Independence and the U. S. Constitution? Or were they just property, like a farmer's oxen? There were other conflicts, too. People in the North and South had different lifestyles and businesses. They also wanted different things from government.

The monster was tearing the country apart. People were fighting-mad and shooting and knifing each other along the border between Missouri and the Kansas Territory. Would Kansas be slave or free? The flames of burning homes and barns lit up the night sky.

War clouds were gathering.

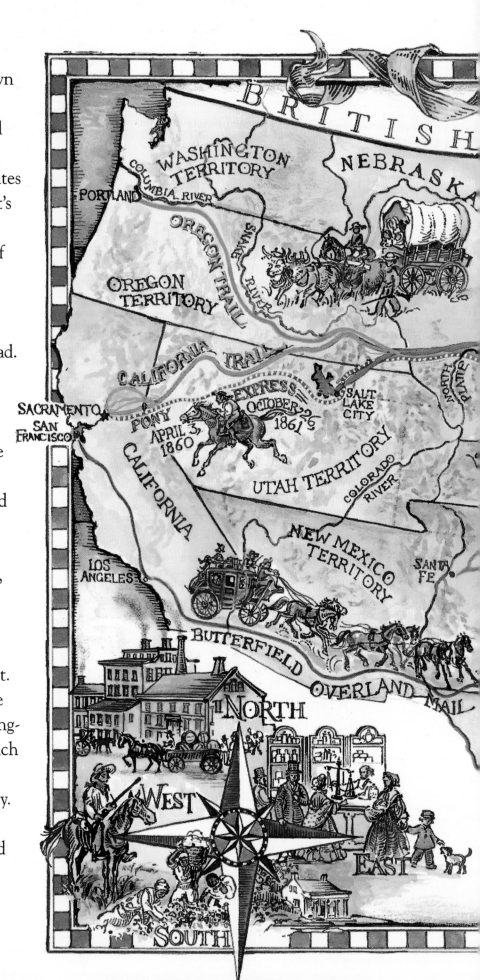

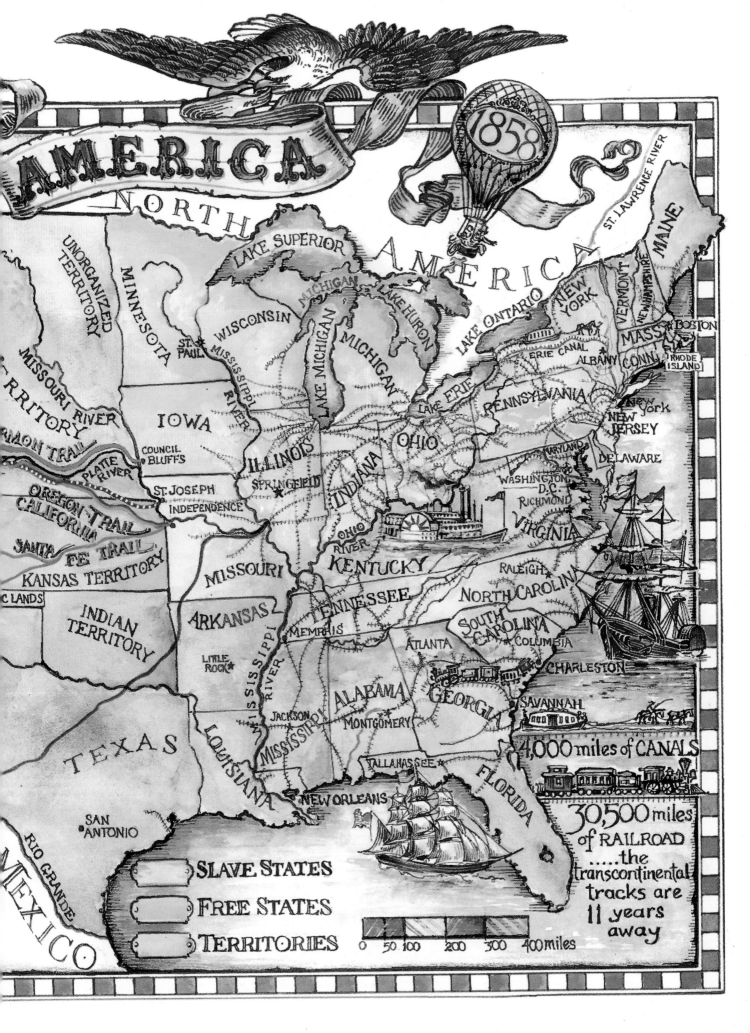

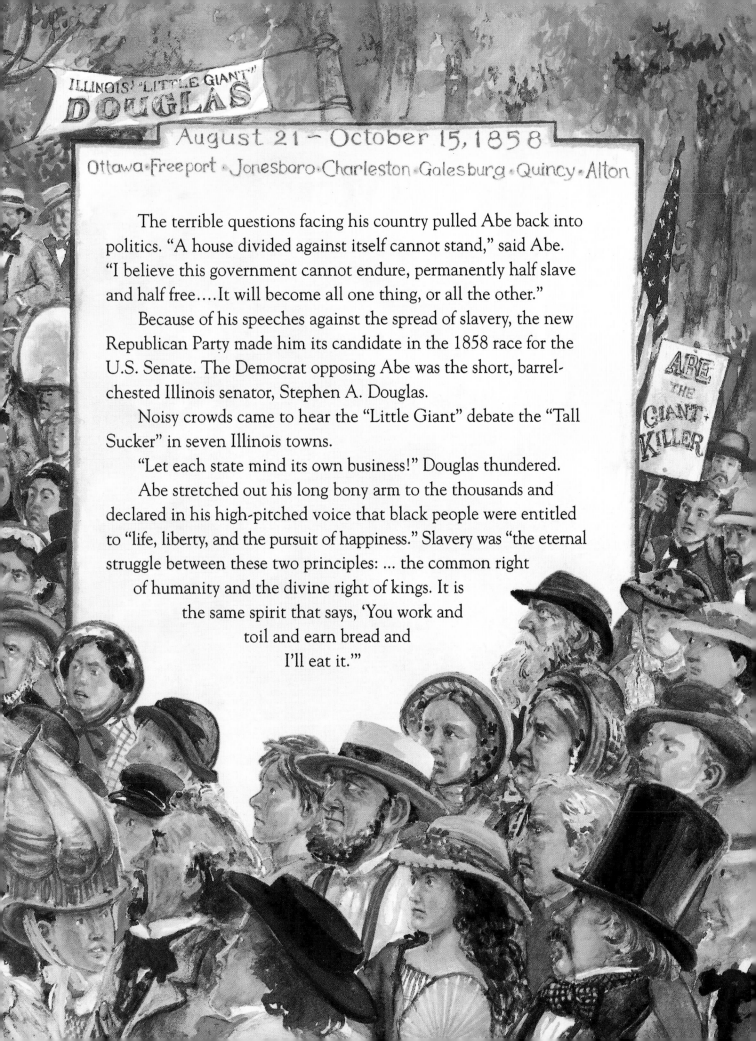

ILLINOIS' "LITTLE GIANT"
DOUGLAS

August 21 – October 15, 1858

Ottawa·Freeport·Jonesboro·Charleston·Galesburg·Quincy·Alton

The terrible questions facing his country pulled Abe back into politics. "A house divided against itself cannot stand," said Abe. "I believe this government cannot endure, permanently half slave and half free....It will become all one thing, or all the other."

Because of his speeches against the spread of slavery, the new Republican Party made him its candidate in the 1858 race for the U.S. Senate. The Democrat opposing Abe was the short, barrel-chested Illinois senator, Stephen A. Douglas.

Noisy crowds came to hear the "Little Giant" debate the "Tall Sucker" in seven Illinois towns.

"Let each state mind its own business!" Douglas thundered.

Abe stretched out his long bony arm to the thousands and declared in his high-pitched voice that black people were entitled to "life, liberty, and the pursuit of happiness." Slavery was "the eternal struggle between these two principles: ... the common right of humanity and the divine right of kings. It is the same spirit that says, 'You work and toil and earn bread and I'll eat it.'"

ABE THE GIANT-KILLER

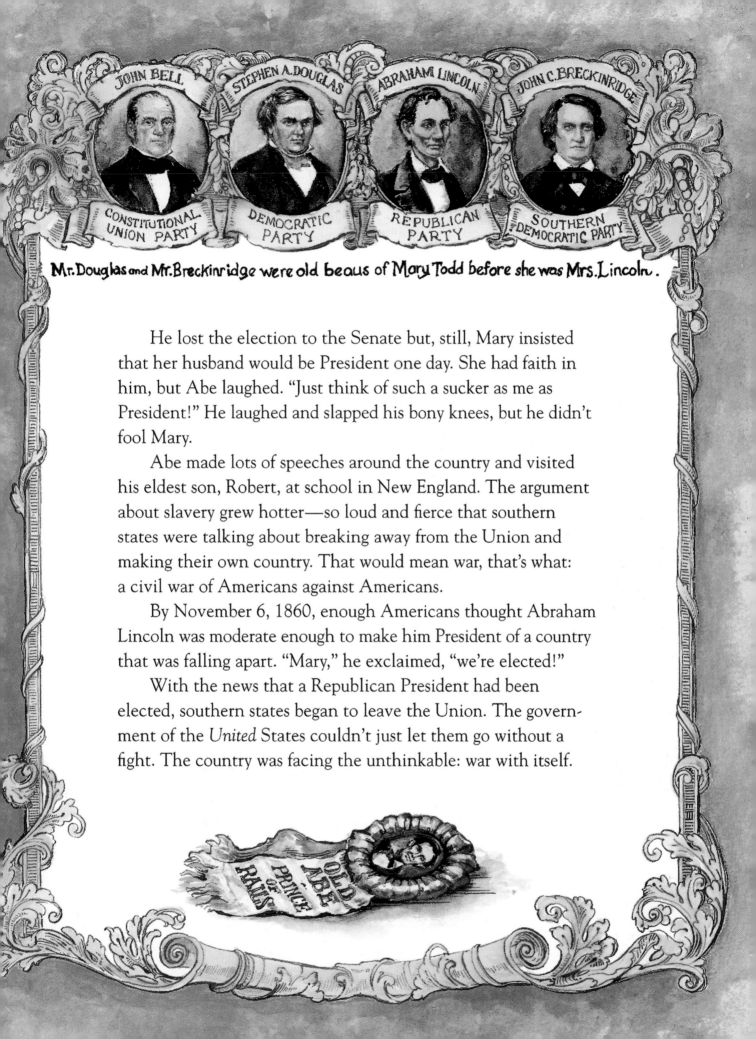

JOHN BELL — CONSTITUTIONAL UNION PARTY

STEPHEN A. DOUGLAS — DEMOCRATIC PARTY

ABRAHAM LINCOLN — REPUBLICAN PARTY

JOHN C. BRECKINRIDGE — SOUTHERN DEMOCRATIC PARTY

Mr. Douglas and Mr. Breckinridge were old beaus of Mary Todd before she was Mrs. Lincoln.

He lost the election to the Senate but, still, Mary insisted that her husband would be President one day. She had faith in him, but Abe laughed. "Just think of such a sucker as me as President!" He laughed and slapped his bony knees, but he didn't fool Mary.

Abe made lots of speeches around the country and visited his eldest son, Robert, at school in New England. The argument about slavery grew hotter—so loud and fierce that southern states were talking about breaking away from the Union and making their own country. That would mean war, that's what: a civil war of Americans against Americans.

By November 6, 1860, enough Americans thought Abraham Lincoln was moderate enough to make him President of a country that was falling apart. "Mary," he exclaimed, "we're elected!"

With the news that a Republican President had been elected, southern states began to leave the Union. The government of the *United* States couldn't just let them go without a fight. The country was facing the unthinkable: war with itself.

OLD ABE PRINCE OF RAILS

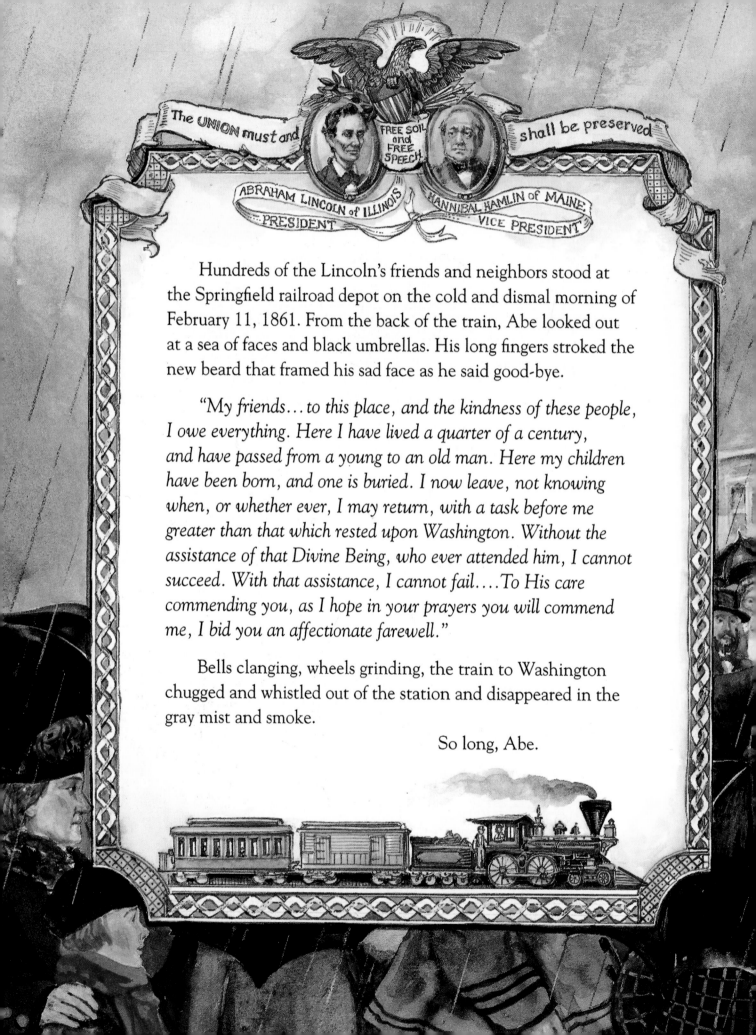

The UNION must and shall be preserved

FREE SOIL and FREE SPEECH

ABRAHAM LINCOLN of ILLINOIS ... PRESIDENT

HANNIBAL HAMLIN of MAINE ... VICE PRESIDENT

Hundreds of the Lincoln's friends and neighbors stood at the Springfield railroad depot on the cold and dismal morning of February 11, 1861. From the back of the train, Abe looked out at a sea of faces and black umbrellas. His long fingers stroked the new beard that framed his sad face as he said good-bye.

"My friends...to this place, and the kindness of these people, I owe everything. Here I have lived a quarter of a century, and have passed from a young to an old man. Here my children have been born, and one is buried. I now leave, not knowing when, or whether ever, I may return, with a task before me greater than that which rested upon Washington. Without the assistance of that Divine Being, who ever attended him, I cannot succeed. With that assistance, I cannot fail....To His care commending you, as I hope in your prayers you will commend me, I bid you an affectionate farewell."

Bells clanging, wheels grinding, the train to Washington chugged and whistled out of the station and disappeared in the gray mist and smoke.

So long, Abe.

Abe got a letter from an 11-year-old girl named Grace Bedell. She suggested that Abe should let his whiskers grow.

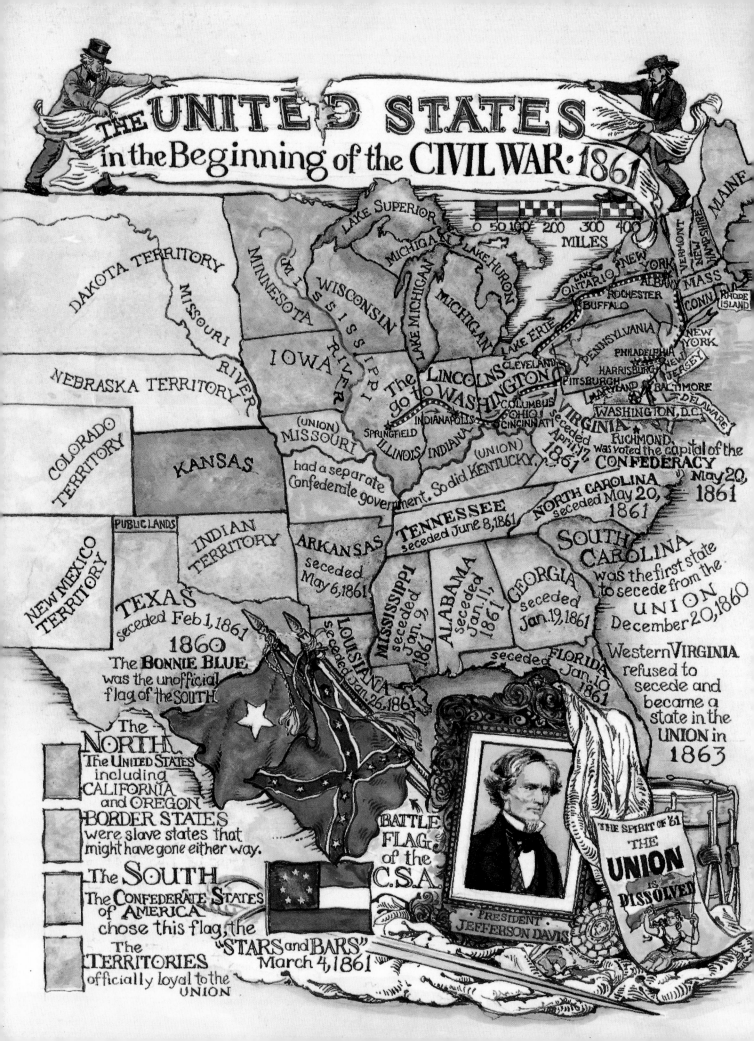

Two days before Abe left Springfield on the train, Jefferson Davis, who had been a U.S. Senator from Mississippi, was elected President of the new Confederacy.

On March 4, 1861, on his Inauguration Day, President Lincoln told the South: "In your hands, my dissatisfied fellow countrymen, and not in mine, is the momentous issue of civil war....We must not be enemies."

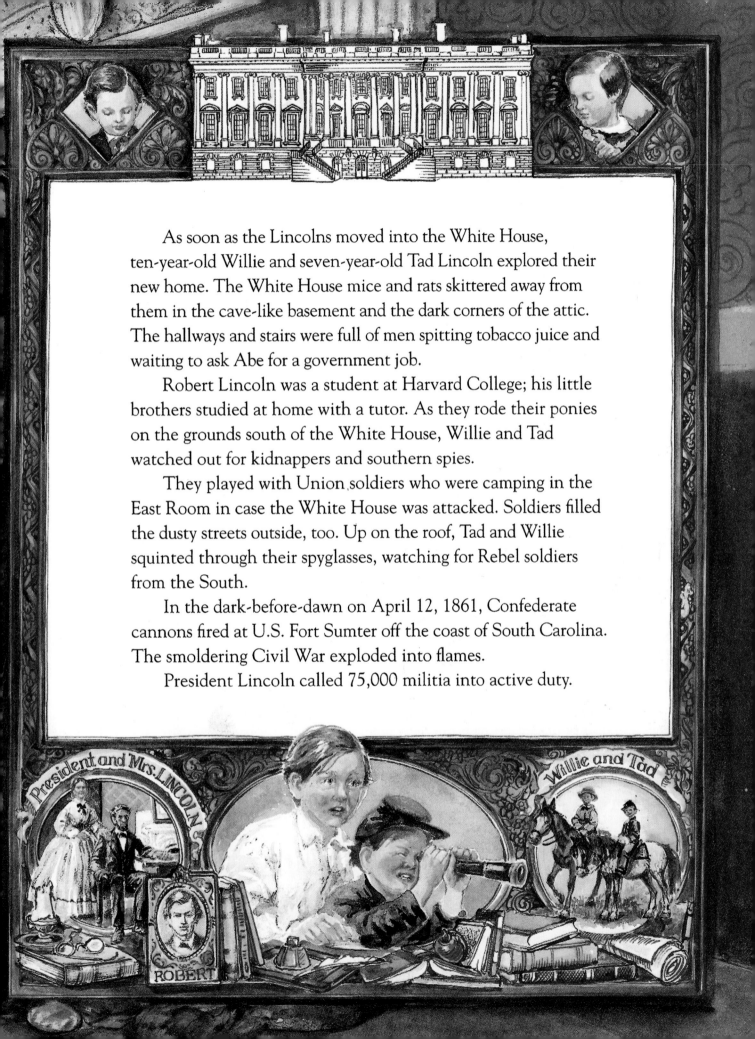

As soon as the Lincolns moved into the White House, ten-year-old Willie and seven-year-old Tad Lincoln explored their new home. The White House mice and rats skittered away from them in the cave-like basement and the dark corners of the attic. The hallways and stairs were full of men spitting tobacco juice and waiting to ask Abe for a government job.

Robert Lincoln was a student at Harvard College; his little brothers studied at home with a tutor. As they rode their ponies on the grounds south of the White House, Willie and Tad watched out for kidnappers and southern spies.

They played with Union soldiers who were camping in the East Room in case the White House was attacked. Soldiers filled the dusty streets outside, too. Up on the roof, Tad and Willie squinted through their spyglasses, watching for Rebel soldiers from the South.

In the dark-before-dawn on April 12, 1861, Confederate cannons fired at U.S. Fort Sumter off the coast of South Carolina. The smoldering Civil War exploded into flames.

President Lincoln called 75,000 militia into active duty.

President and Mrs. LINCOLN

ROBERT

Willie and Tad

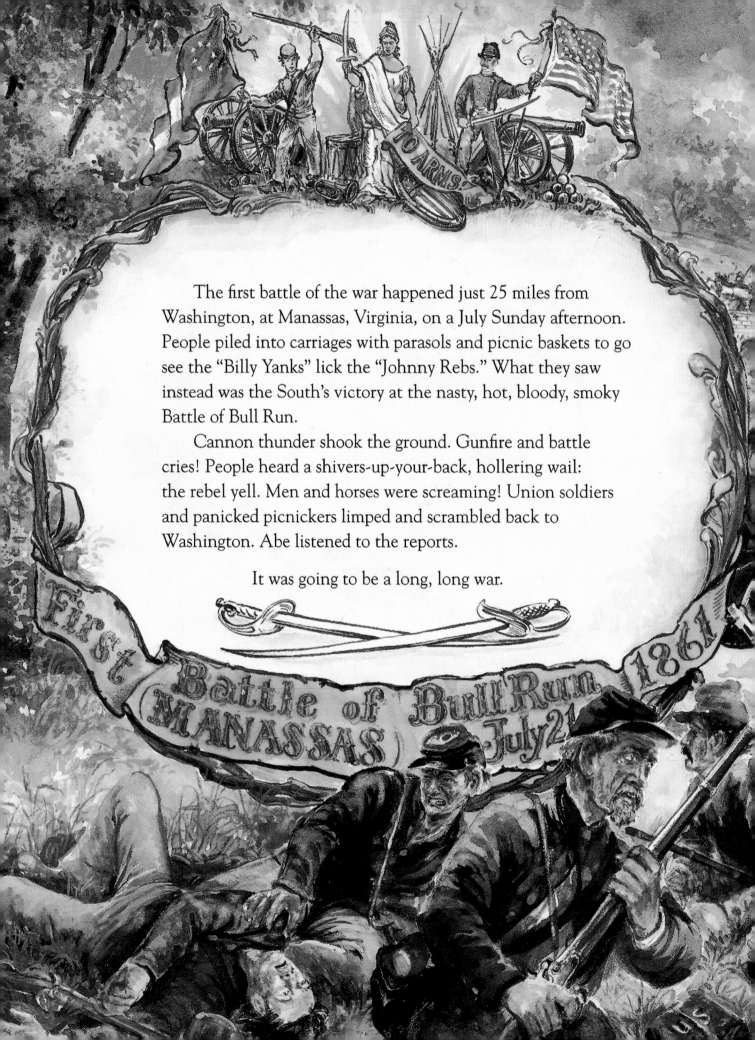

The first battle of the war happened just 25 miles from Washington, at Manassas, Virginia, on a July Sunday afternoon. People piled into carriages with parasols and picnic baskets to go see the "Billy Yanks" lick the "Johnny Rebs." What they saw instead was the South's victory at the nasty, hot, bloody, smoky Battle of Bull Run.

Cannon thunder shook the ground. Gunfire and battle cries! People heard a shivers-up-your-back, hollering wail: the rebel yell. Men and horses were screaming! Union soldiers and panicked picnickers limped and scrambled back to Washington. Abe listened to the reports.

It was going to be a long, long war.

First Battle of Bull Run (MANASSAS) July 21 1861

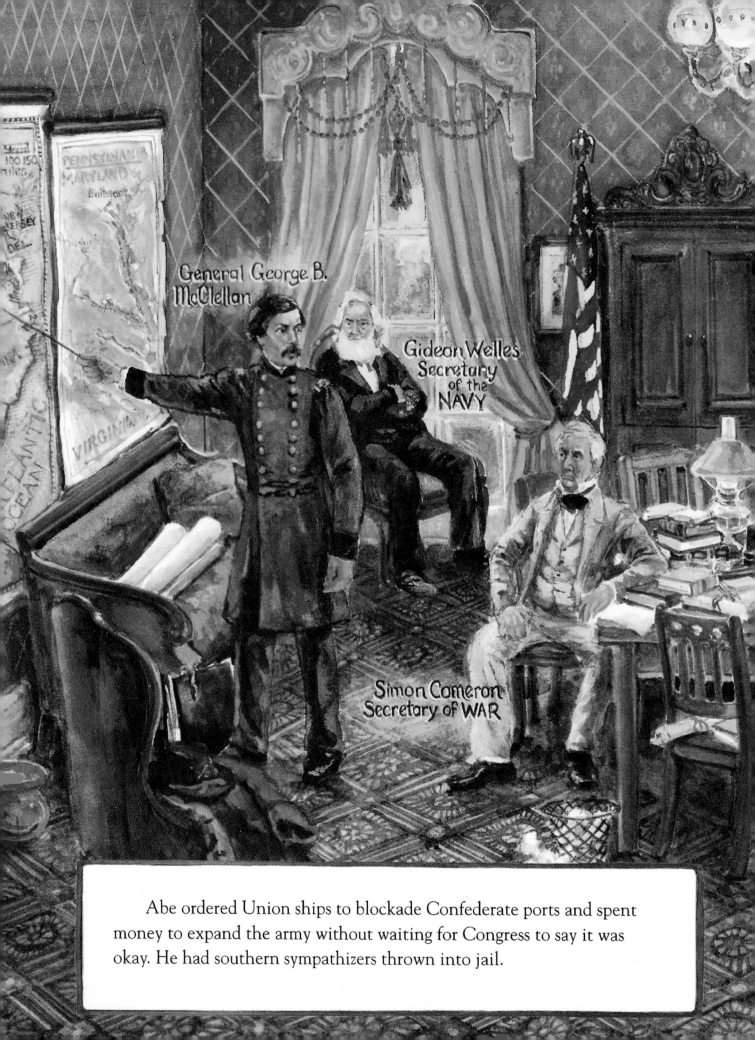

Abe ordered Union ships to blockade Confederate ports and spent money to expand the army without waiting for Congress to say it was okay. He had southern sympathizers thrown into jail.

President LINCOLN

John G. Nicolay Secretary to the President

John Hay other Secretary to the President

William H. Seward Secretary of STATE

He made 35-year-old George McClellan the commanding general of his army. People said McClellan was a military genius, and "Little Mac", as he was known, agreed. The President was determined to put down the rebellion and save the Union, no matter what.

Outside the White House, the weather grew cold and gray as 1861 came to an end. General McClellan drilled his Union soldiers in the mud. Inside, Tad and Willie were sick. Tad got better, but Willie grew worse and worse until he died. Abe looked down at Willie's pale still face and cried. He said softly, "It is hard, hard, hard to have him die."

Mary Lincoln wept and tried to talk to Willie's ghost late at night after night while Abe worked on, his sadness for his boy and for all the boys hurt and dying in battle all mixed together.

Abe studied books about the art of war and military strategy. He studied the varnished paper maps that lined the walls of his office, and visited the battlefields and hospitals. The Civil War had spread from the Atlantic Ocean to beyond the Mississippi River.

Abe grew frustrated with General McClellan who was painfully slow to attack, then let Confederate armies and victories get away.

The general privately called the President a "well-meaning baboon."

The North needed to win the war, or the Nation of 1776 would be lost forever. The North needed a new strategy. The President knew that European nations might side with the South for business reasons, but they would never get involved in a war about slavery.

Abraham Lincoln issued his Emancipation Proclamation on September 22, 1862.

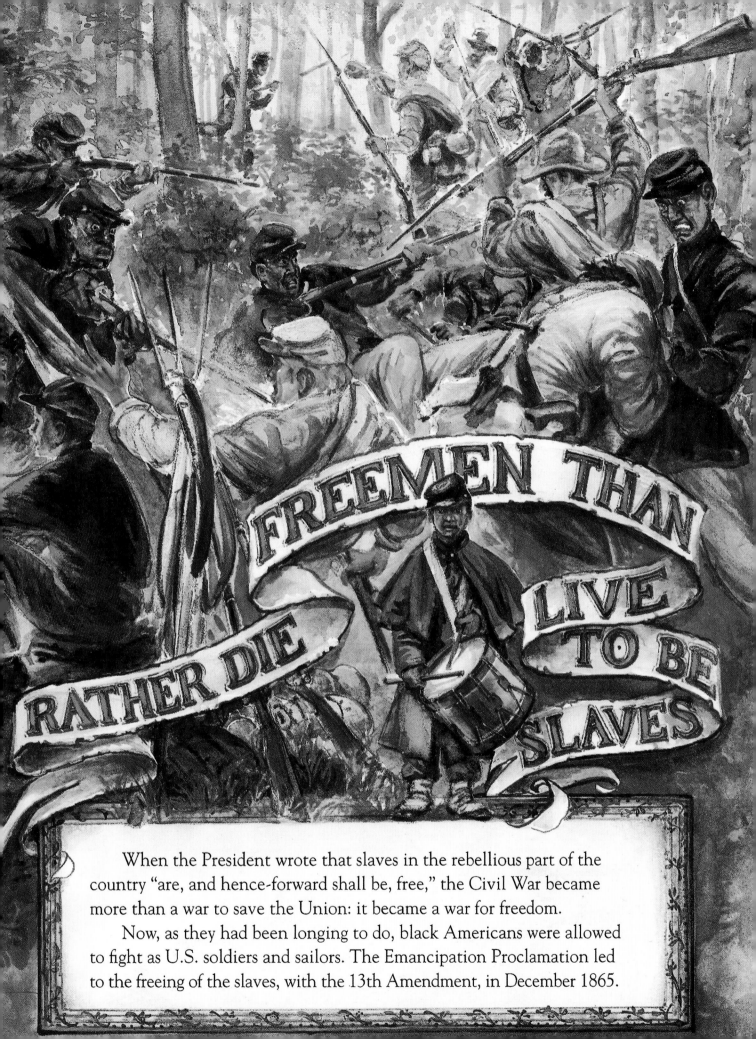

FREEMEN THAN

RATHER DIE

LIVE TO BE SLAVES

When the President wrote that slaves in the rebellious part of the country "are, and hence-forward shall be, free," the Civil War became more than a war to save the Union: it became a war for freedom.

Now, as they had been longing to do, black Americans were allowed to fight as U.S. soldiers and sailors. The Emancipation Proclamation led to the freeing of the slaves, with the 13th Amendment, in December 1865.

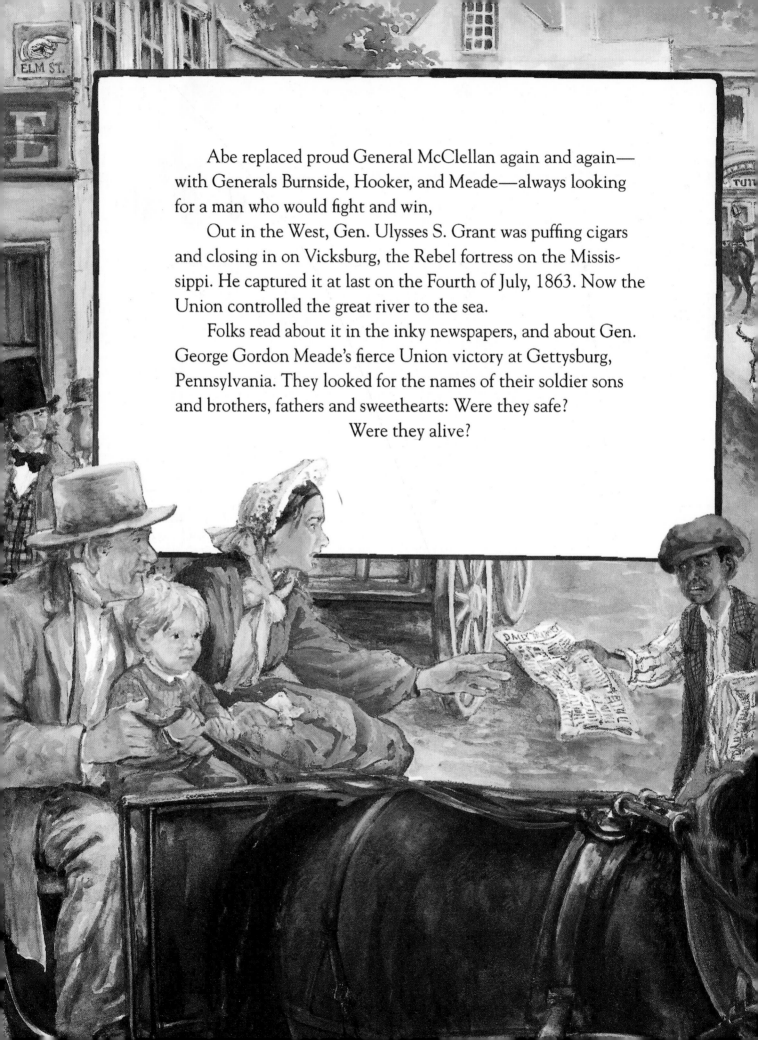

Abe replaced proud General McClellan again and again—
with Generals Burnside, Hooker, and Meade—always looking
for a man who would fight and win,

Out in the West, Gen. Ulysses S. Grant was puffing cigars
and closing in on Vicksburg, the Rebel fortress on the Mississippi. He captured it at last on the Fourth of July, 1863. Now the
Union controlled the great river to the sea.

Folks read about it in the inky newspapers, and about Gen.
George Gordon Meade's fierce Union victory at Gettysburg,
Pennsylvania. They looked for the names of their soldier sons
and brothers, fathers and sweethearts: Were they safe?

Were they alive?

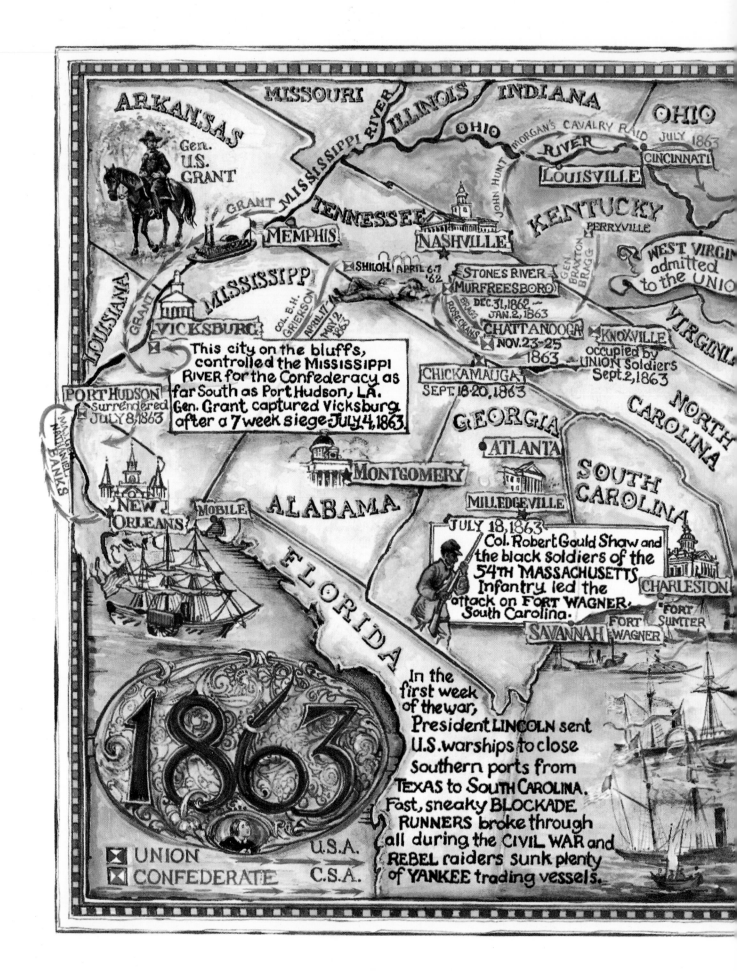

MISSOURI

ILLINOIS

INDIANA

ARKANSAS

OHIO

OHIO

Gen. U.S. GRANT

MISSISSIPPI RIVER

MORGAN'S CAVALRY RAID

JULY 1863

CINCINNATI

GRANT

JOHN HUNT

RIVER

LOUISVILLE

KENTUCKY

TENNESSEE

MEMPHIS

NASHVILLE

PERRYVILLE

WEST VIRGINIA
admitted
to the UNION

LOUISIANA

MISSISSIPPI

SHILOH APRIL 6.7 '62

STONES RIVER
MURFREESBORO

GEN. BRAXTON BRAGG

VIRGINIA

GRANT

VICKSBURG

COL. B.H. GRIERSON
APRIL 17

MAY 12 1863

DEC.31,1862 —
JAN.2,1863

BRAGG
ROSE CRANS

CHATTANOOGA
NOV.23-25
1863

KNOXVILLE
occupied by
UNION Soldiers
Sept.2, 1863

This city on the bluffs,
controlled the MISSISSIPPI
RIVER for the Confederacy as
far South as Port Hudson, LA.
Gen. Grant captured Vicksburg
after a 7 week siege July 4, 1863.

CHICKAMAUGA
SEPT.18-20, 1863

NORTH
CAROLINA

PORT HUDSON
surrendered
JULY 8, 1863

GEORGIA

ATLANTA

MAJ. GENERAL NATHANIEL BANKS

MONTGOMERY

ALABAMA

MILLEDGEVILLE

SOUTH
CAROLINA

NEW
ORLEANS

MOBILE

JULY 18, 1863
Col. Robert Gould Shaw and
the black soldiers of the
54TH MASSACHUSETTS
Infantry led the
attack on FORT WAGNER,
South Carolina.

CHARLESTON

FLORIDA

FORT
WAGNER

FORT
SUMTER

SAVANNAH

In the
first week
of the war,
President LINCOLN sent
U.S. warships to close
Southern ports from
TEXAS to SOUTH CAROLINA.
Fast, sneaky BLOCKADE
RUNNERS broke through
all during the CIVIL WAR and
REBEL raiders sunk plenty
of YANKEE trading vessels.

1863

☒ UNION   U.S.A.
☒ CONFEDERATE   C.S.A.

After the CONFEDERATE victory at CHANCELLORSVILLE, Pres. JEFFERSON DAVIS and Gen. ROBERT E. LEE decided to invade the NORTH. LEE's ARMY of Northern VIRGINIA met UNION Gen. GEORGE GORDON MEADE and the U.S. ARMY of the POTOMAC in the town of GETTYSBURG in southern PENNSYLVANIA. They met in the greatest battle ever fought in the WESTERN HEMISPHERE.

An army of 90,000 Union soldiers faced 75,000 soldiers of the South for three hot days in the bloodiest battle of the war. Even when all the young men's grand-babies were in the ground, people would still talk about the brave and terrible fighting at Gettysburg. More than 50,000 men were hurt, missing, or killed. Robert E. Lee's defeated forces headed across the Potomac River, back into Virginia.

Abe slapped his big hand on his desk with frustration. Union General Meade had not chased the retreating Rebel soldiers and licked them once and for all. "We had them within our grasp," said the grim, tired President.

The war might have ended, but now it would go on.

And on.

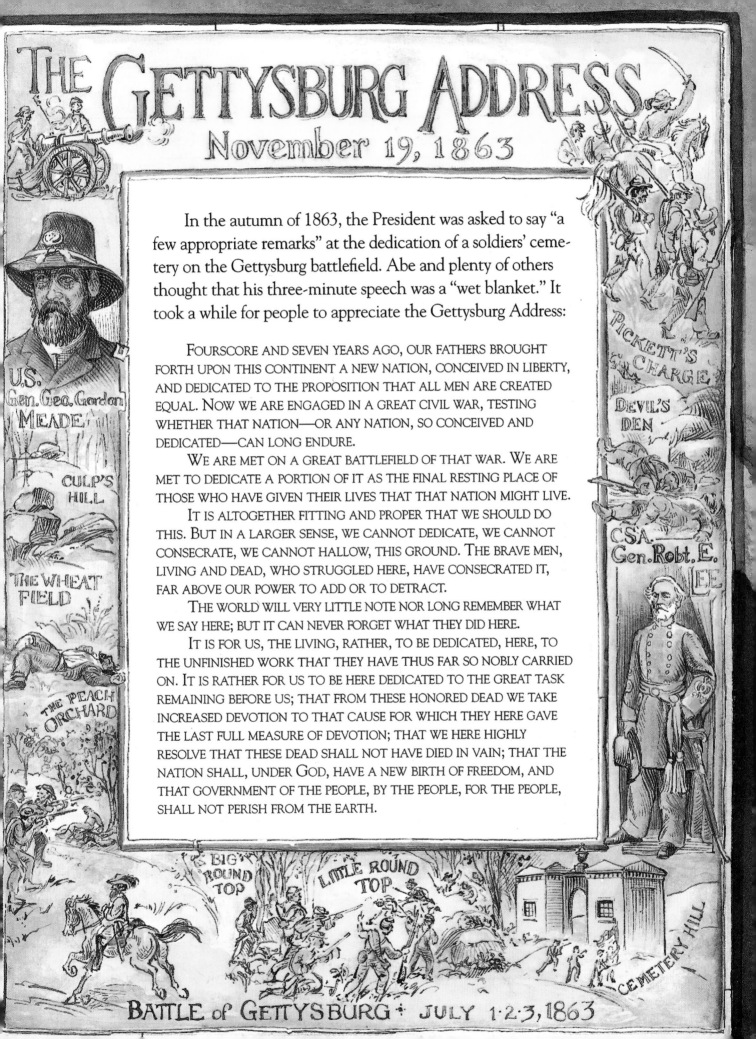

THE GETTYSBURG ADDRESS
November 19, 1863

In the autumn of 1863, the President was asked to say "a few appropriate remarks" at the dedication of a soldiers' cemetery on the Gettysburg battlefield. Abe and plenty of others thought that his three-minute speech was a "wet blanket." It took a while for people to appreciate the Gettysburg Address:

FOURSCORE AND SEVEN YEARS AGO, OUR FATHERS BROUGHT FORTH UPON THIS CONTINENT A NEW NATION, CONCEIVED IN LIBERTY, AND DEDICATED TO THE PROPOSITION THAT ALL MEN ARE CREATED EQUAL. NOW WE ARE ENGAGED IN A GREAT CIVIL WAR, TESTING WHETHER THAT NATION—OR ANY NATION, SO CONCEIVED AND DEDICATED—CAN LONG ENDURE.

WE ARE MET ON A GREAT BATTLEFIELD OF THAT WAR. WE ARE MET TO DEDICATE A PORTION OF IT AS THE FINAL RESTING PLACE OF THOSE WHO HAVE GIVEN THEIR LIVES THAT THAT NATION MIGHT LIVE.

IT IS ALTOGETHER FITTING AND PROPER THAT WE SHOULD DO THIS. BUT IN A LARGER SENSE, WE CANNOT DEDICATE, WE CANNOT CONSECRATE, WE CANNOT HALLOW, THIS GROUND. THE BRAVE MEN, LIVING AND DEAD, WHO STRUGGLED HERE, HAVE CONSECRATED IT, FAR ABOVE OUR POWER TO ADD OR TO DETRACT.

THE WORLD WILL VERY LITTLE NOTE NOR LONG REMEMBER WHAT WE SAY HERE; BUT IT CAN NEVER FORGET WHAT THEY DID HERE.

IT IS FOR US, THE LIVING, RATHER, TO BE DEDICATED, HERE, TO THE UNFINISHED WORK THAT THEY HAVE THUS FAR SO NOBLY CARRIED ON. IT IS RATHER FOR US TO BE HERE DEDICATED TO THE GREAT TASK REMAINING BEFORE US; THAT FROM THESE HONORED DEAD WE TAKE INCREASED DEVOTION TO THAT CAUSE FOR WHICH THEY HERE GAVE THE LAST FULL MEASURE OF DEVOTION; THAT WE HERE HIGHLY RESOLVE THAT THESE DEAD SHALL NOT HAVE DIED IN VAIN; THAT THE NATION SHALL, UNDER GOD, HAVE A NEW BIRTH OF FREEDOM, AND THAT GOVERNMENT OF THE PEOPLE, BY THE PEOPLE, FOR THE PEOPLE, SHALL NOT PERISH FROM THE EARTH.

U.S. Gen. Geo. Gordon MEADE

CULP'S HILL

THE WHEAT FIELD

THE PEACH ORCHARD

PICKETT'S CHARGE

DEVIL'S DEN

CSA. Gen. Robt. E. LEE

BIG ROUND TOP

LITTLE ROUND TOP

CEMETERY HILL

BATTLE OF GETTYSBURG • JULY 1·2·3, 1863

PRESIDENT
Abraham Lincoln

VICE PRESIDENT
Andrew Johnson

UNION

1864

Ulysses S. Grant was the Union's top general now, in March of 1864. Thousands and thousands of soldiers died as Grant and his men pushed on against Gen. Robert E. Lee and his troops. When would the fighting end? And how in the world could a President get re-elected in the middle of a civil war that everybody was sick of?

"Sometimes," Abe said, "I'm the tiredest man on earth." When the votes were counted in 1864, Abe won a second term in office. The Democrat he defeated was his former commanding general, George McClellan.

At his second Inauguration, March 4, 1865, Abraham Lincoln said these words:

WITH MALICE TOWARD NONE;
WITH CHARITY FOR ALL; WITH FIRMNESS IN THE RIGHT,
AS GOD GIVES US TO SEE THE RIGHT, LET US STRIVE ON TO FINISH
THE WORK WE ARE IN; TO BIND UP THE NATION'S WOUNDS,
TO CARE FOR HIM WHO SHALL HAVE BORNE THE BATTLE,
AND FOR HIS WIDOW, AND HIS ORPHAN—TO DO ALL WHICH MAY
ACHIEVE AND CHERISH A JUST, AND A LASTING PEACE,
AMONG OURSELVES, AND WITH ALL NATIONS.

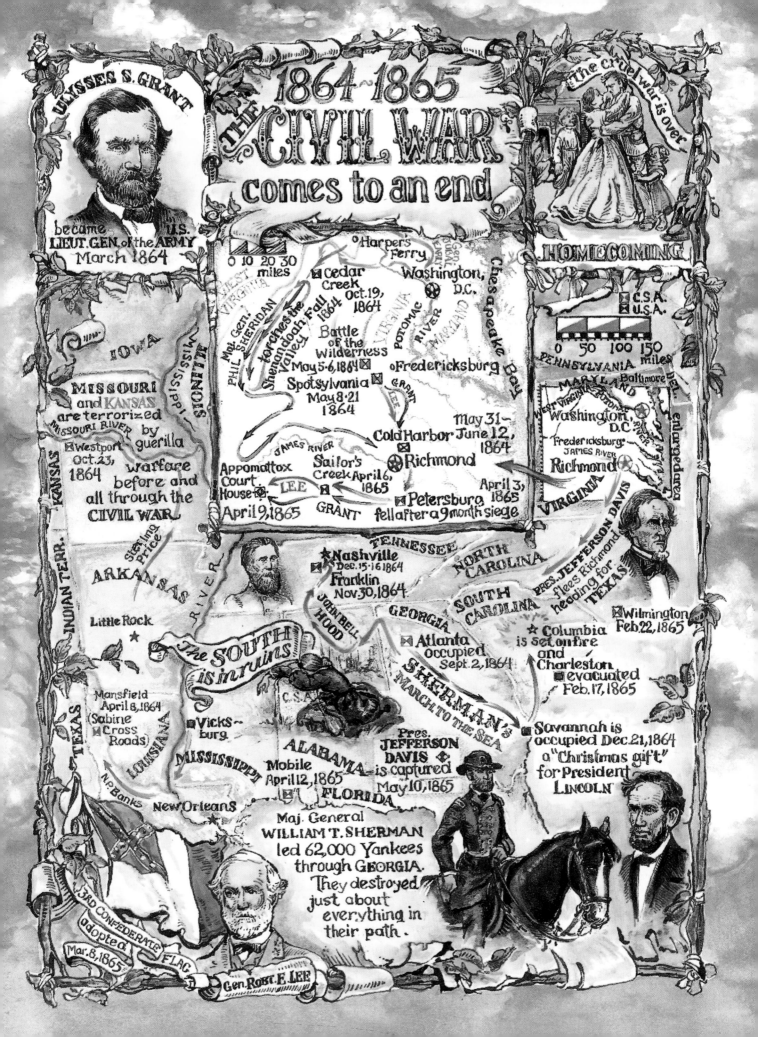

The Union soldiers captured the Confederate capital, Richmond, Virginia, on April 3, 1865. The very next day, Abe and Tad went there on a small boat. Wrecked ships and dead horses floated in the water. Black people came to greet the President as he walked through the burnt city. Pale faces watched from the windows. Abe sat for a moment at Jefferson Davis's desk.

"What about these conquered people?" the President was asked.

"Let 'em up easy," Abe sighed.

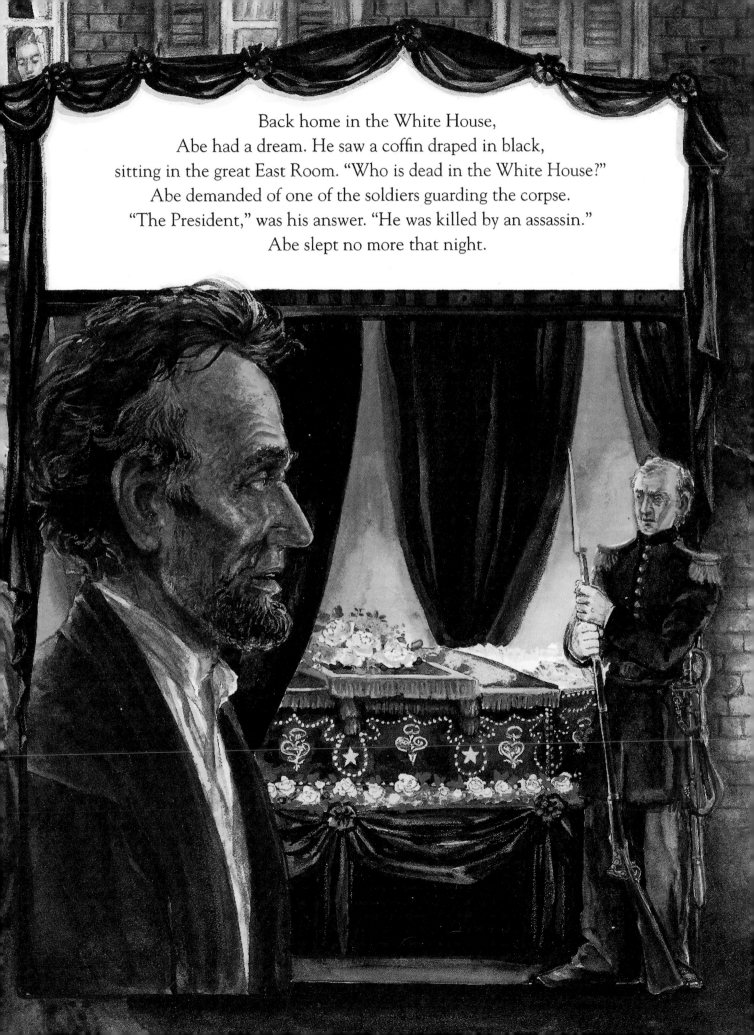

Back home in the White House,
Abe had a dream. He saw a coffin draped in black,
sitting in the great East Room. "Who is dead in the White House?"
Abe demanded of one of the soldiers guarding the corpse.
"The President," was his answer. "He was killed by an assassin."
Abe slept no more that night.

1865

General Lee surrendered his gallant, tattered army to General Grant on April 9, 1865, at Appomattox Courthouse, in Virginia. The war was over at last. More than 2,300,000 men had fought in the many battles. Now soldiers were marching home.

In front of the White House, a band was playing. Crowds of people were yelling and throwing hundreds of hats high into the air. Abe went out to greet them all. Mischievous Tad waved a captured battle flag of the Confederacy from the White House window. When Abe saw it, his tired face crinkled into a smile. "Play 'Dixie,'" Abe said to the band. "It's one of the best tunes I've ever heard."

Major struggled with Mr. Booth and got stabbed with the actor's dagger! As Booth jumped to the stage, he shouted, "Sic semper tyrannis!" (Thus always to tyrants!), then broke his ankle when he landed on the stage. Booth was caught and killed 12 days later. Eight other people who helped Booth were later hanged or put in prison. Abe and Mary Lincoln were accompanied by Major Rathbone and his fiancée, Clara Harris. After Abe was shot, the young

Mr. Booth's Gun
(2/3 its actual size)

Friday evening five days later, Abe took Mary to see a funny play at Ford's Theatre.

"We must both be more cheerful," said Abe. "Between the war and the loss of our darling Willie, we have both been very miserable."

That night, an actor who was full of whiskey and anger about the way the war had turned out, sneaked into the box where the Lincolns and their guests were sitting. John Wilkes Booth shot his small pistol, leaped from the box onto the stage, then ran to the back of the theater and into the night.

He escaped on a galloping horse—for a time.

"NO! *Oh, no!* The President's been shot!" The theater was full of screaming. "Mr. Lincoln's been shot!"

Abe was carried across the street to a little room in a boarding house. That was where he died the next morning, April 15, 1865. His body was carried back to the White House to lay in state in the East Room.

Soldiers stood watch as 25,000 people slowly walked past Abe's black-draped coffin.

Never before had an American President been murdered. In the aftermath of the shooting, John Wilkes Booth was killed and those who plotted with him to kill the President were hanged or put in prison. Vice President Andrew Johnson became the 17th President, as the 16th became a legend.

The tall, skinny, poor boy, the frontier tree-chopper, the flatboat man with only a year of proper school, the village shopkeeper and country lawyer became "Father Abraham, the Emancipator," the President who saved the Union.

A funeral train carried Abe Lincoln back to Springfield, Illinois. All along the way, people paid their respects with poems and flowers. In between the towns and cities, people stood along the tracks listening for the lonesome whistle of the funeral train. They stood silently as President Lincoln's train passed by.

So long, Abe.

BIBLIOGRAPHY

Lorant, Stefan. *Lincoln: A Picture Story of His Life.*
New York: W.W. Norton & Company, Inc., 1969.
McPherson, James M. *Battle Cry of Freedom: The Civil War Era.*
New York: Oxford University Press, 1988.
Sandburg, Carl. *Abraham Lincoln: The Prairie Years & The War Years.*
New York: Harcourt Brace, 1926.
Catton, Bruce and Editors: American Heritage. *The American Heritage
Picture History of the Civil War.* New York: 1960.

Copyright © 1997 Cheryl Harness
First paperback edition 2002

Published by the National Geographic Society.

Library of Congress Cataloging-in-Publication Data
Harness, Cheryl.
Abe Lincoln goes to Washington, 1837-1865 / written and illustrated by Cheryl Harness.
p. cm.
Includes bibliographical references.
Summary: Portrays Lincoln's life as a lawyer in Springfield, a devoted husband and father,
and president during the Civil War years.
ISBN 0-7922-3736-6 (hardcover) ISBN: 0-7922-6906-3 (paperback)
1. Lincoln, Abraham, 1809-1865—Juvenile literature. 2. Presidents—United States—
Biography—Juvenile literature. [1. Lincoln, Abraham, 1809-1865. 2. Presidents.] I. Title.
E457.905.H296 1996
973.7'092—dc20   96-9587
[B]

Printed in the United States

One of the world's largest nonprofit scientific and educational organizations, the National Geographic Society was founded in 1888 "for the increase and
diffusion of geographic knowledge." Fulfilling this mission, the Society educates and inspires millions every day through its magazines, books, television
programs, videos, maps and atlases, research grants, the National Geographic Bee, teacher workshops, and innovative classroom materials. The Society
is supported through membership dues, charitable gifts, and income from the sale of its educational products. This support is vital to National
Geographic's mission to increase global understanding and promote conservation of our planet through exploration, research, and education.

For more information, please call 1-800-NGS LINE (647-5463) or write to the
following address:

NATIONAL GEOGRAPHIC SOCIETY
1145 17th Street N.W.
Washington, D.C. 20036-4688 U.S.A.

Visit the Society's Web site: www.nationalgeographic.com